PIGGLES' GUIDE TO...

SPACE SHUTTLES

BY KIRSTY HOLMES

THE SECRET BOOK COMPANY

©2019
The Secret Book Company
King's Lynn
Norfolk PE30 4LS

ISBN: 978-1-912502-52-3

Written by:
Kirsty Holmes
Edited by:
John Wood
Designed by:
Danielle Rippengill

A catalogue record for this book
is available from the British Library.

All facts, statistics, web addresses and URLs in this book were verified as valid and accurate at time of writing.
No responsibility for any changes to external websites or references can be accepted by either the author or publisher.

Original idea by Harrison Holmes.

IMAGE CREDITS

CONTENTS

WORDS THAT LOOK LIKE this CAN BE FOUND IN THE GLOSSARY ON PAGE 24.

WELCOME TO FLIGHT SCHOOL!

So you're interested in space shuttles? Do you dream of zooming through the stars in a giant rocket? Then you've come to the right place! The Sty in the Sky Flight School!

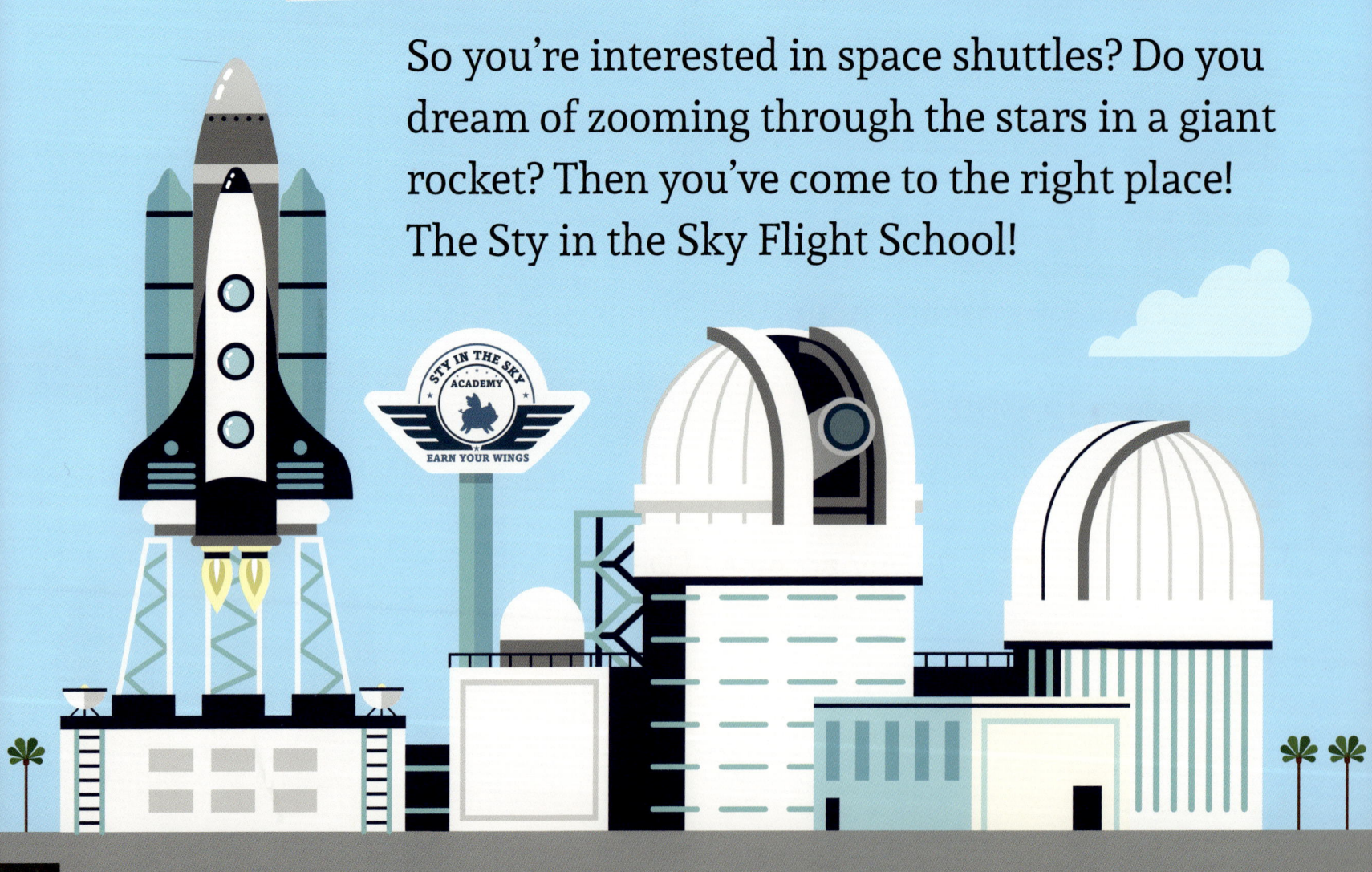

Here, you will learn all you need to know about some amazing spacecrafts, and join the **elite** space force known as the Pink Wings! So pay attention: it's time to FLY!

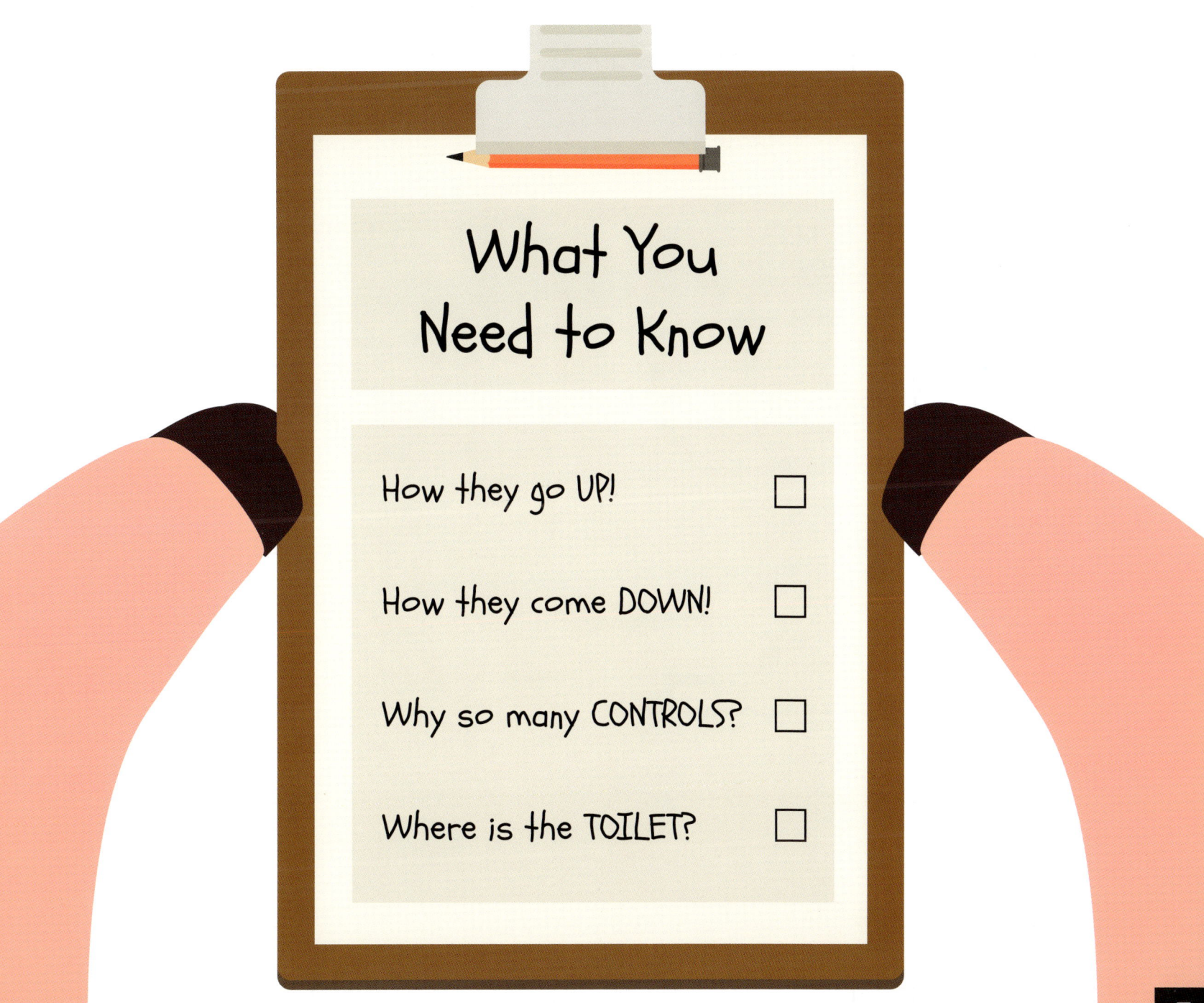

What You Need to Know

How they go UP! ☐

How they come DOWN! ☐

Why so many CONTROLS? ☐

Where is the TOILET? ☐

Lesson 1: WHAT IS A SPACE SHUTTLE?

SPACE SHUTTLE

LAUNCH PAD

Space shuttles are a type of spacecraft. This means they can leave Earth's **atmosphere** and explore space.

Shuttles are used to transport important equipment and highly-trained **astronauts**.

LOTS OF PEOPLE COME TO WATCH SPACE SHUTTLES TAKE OFF.

5...4...3...2...1...TAKE OFF

Space shuttles taking off are VERY LOUD! CAN YOU HEAR ME?!

PARTS OF A SPACE SHUTTLE

U.S. SHUTTLES AND RUSSIAN SHUTTLES LOOK DIFFERENT BUT WORK THE SAME WAY.

FUEL TANK

The huge tank on the shuttle holds the fuel the rocket boosters use.

FLIGHT DECK

The crew can operate the orbiter from here.

PAYLOAD BAY

Anything the shuttle carries, like cargo, is called payload, and is stored here.

ENGINES

The engines move and steer the shuttle in space.

Let's look at the parts of a space shuttle.

ORBITER

The section that carries the passengers, astronauts and anything they have brought with them.

ROCKET BOOSTERS

These lift the shuttle off the ground and blast it into space.

LESSON 3: INSIDE A SPACE SHUTTLE

The flight deck is where the pilots fly the shuttle. All the controls needed to **manoeuvre** (say: man-oo-ver) the shuttle are here. There are over 2,020 controls and displays on the flight deck!

The orbiter also holds the living quarters for the crew. Crew sleep, eat, exercise and even go to the bathroom here. Astronauts have to use special space toilets – it's hard to pee when there is no **gravity**!

LESSON 4:
THRUST!

To get a shuttle into space, you need thrust. Thrust is a **force** which pushes the shuttle straight up, fast enough to escape Earth's gravity and get into space.

DOWN!

Gas escaping from the fuel tanks very quickly is forced DOWN into the ground.

UP!

This downwards force is big enough to push the shuttle UP!

It takes 8 seconds to reach 160 kilometres per hour (kph).

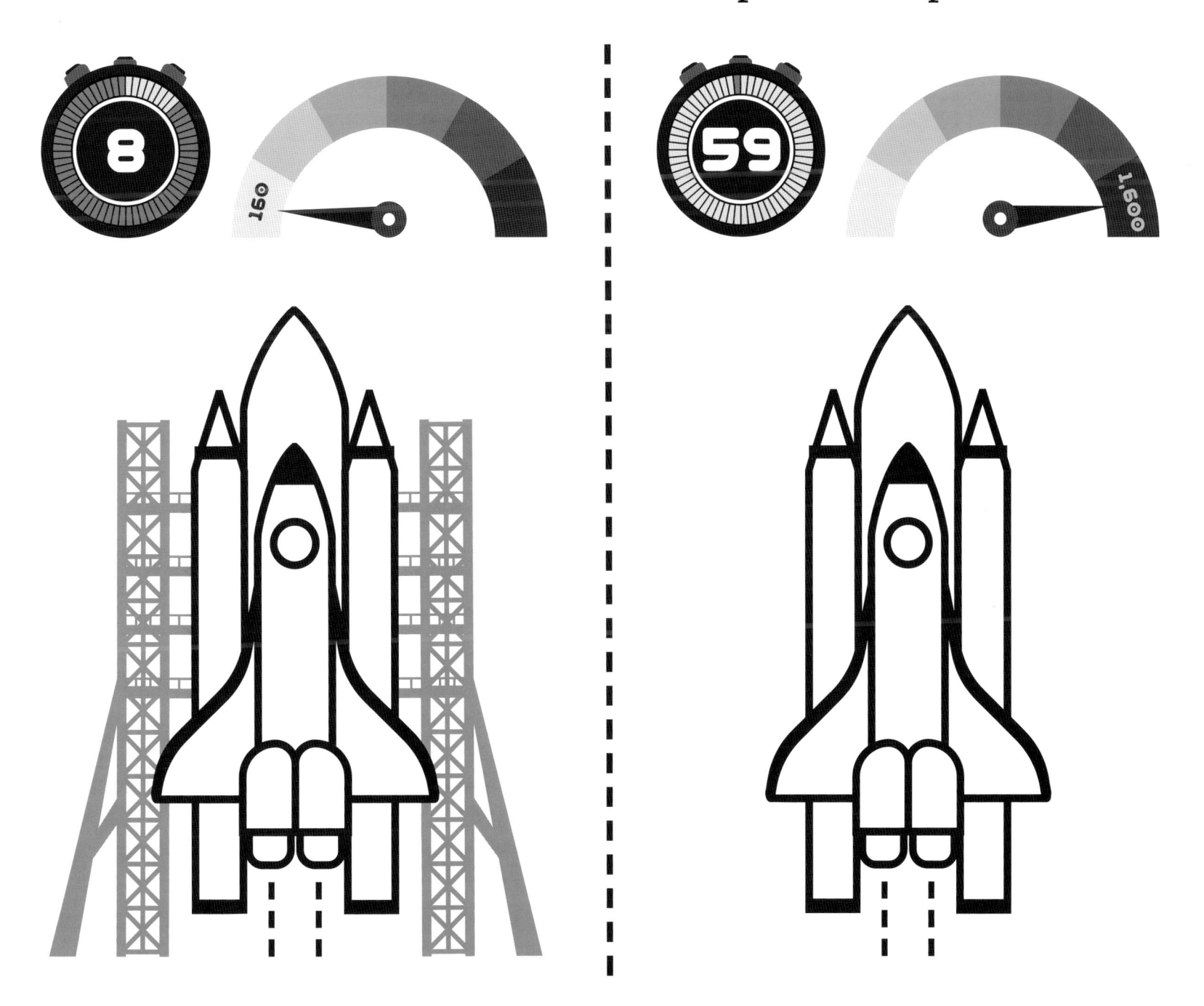

As the fuel is used up, the shuttle gets lighter, and so faster. After a minute, the shuttle is travelling at over 1,600 kph!

LESSON 5:
ORBIT!

After launch, the orbiter drops the tanks and boosters into the sea. This makes the shuttle lighter and easier to steer. The shuttle carries on into space using its own engines.

The shuttle goes into Low-Earth Orbit (LEO). This means it follows a regular, repeating path, quite close to Earth. It travels at around 27,000 kph to stay in orbit.

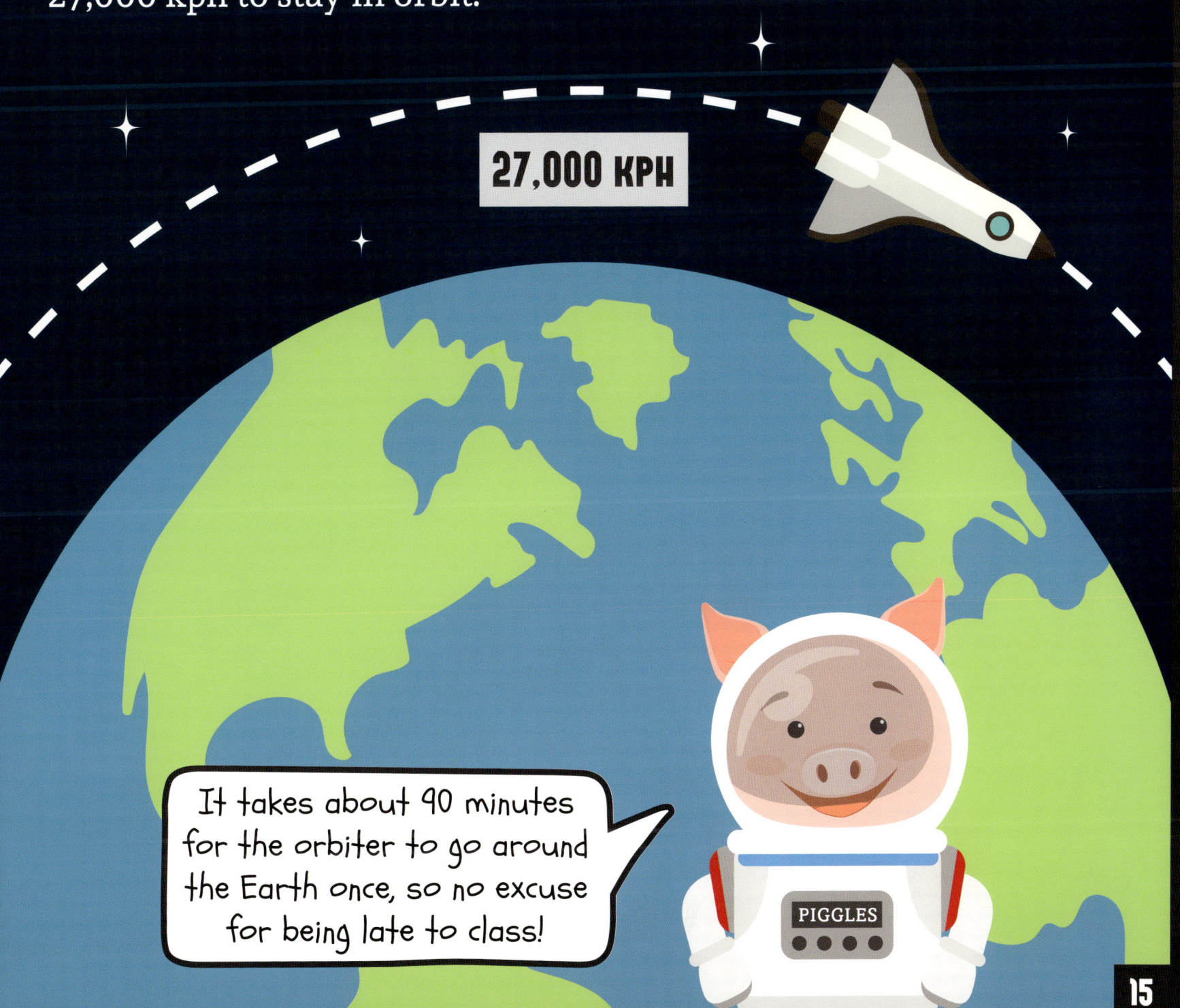

27,000 KPH

It takes about 90 minutes for the orbiter to go around the Earth once, so no excuse for being late to class!

PIGGLES

LESSON 6:
RE-ENTRY AND LANDING

To get back to Earth, the shuttle slows its speed. When it hits the atmosphere, it produces **air resistance** by flying with its nose up – almost like a belly-flop back to Earth!

PIGGLES

The air resistance slows the shuttle down. It gets very hot during re-entry!

Once through the atmosphere, the shuttle can behave like a regular aeroplane, landing on a runway. Computers usually control re-entry and the pilot takes over to land the shuttle.

17

LESSON 7:
FAMOUS SPACE SHUTTLES

COLUMBIA

On April 12th, 1981, NASA launched their first shuttle at Cape Canaveral. The shuttle, Columbia, was piloted by John Young and Robert Crippen.

VALENTINA TERESHKOVA

In 1963, Valentina Tereshkova became the first woman to fly in space. She piloted the Vostok 6.

HUBBLE TELESCOPE

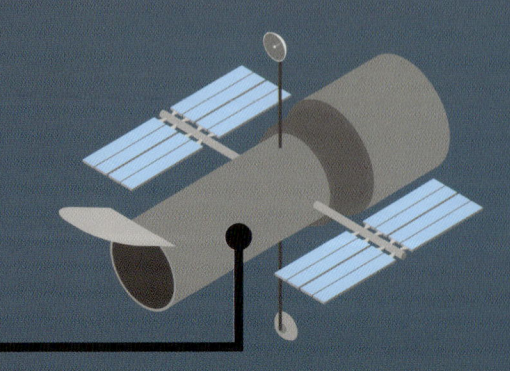

On April 24th, 1990 the shuttle Discovery took the famous Hubble Telescope into orbit.

FIRST ROCKET TO LAND AND BE USED AGAIN

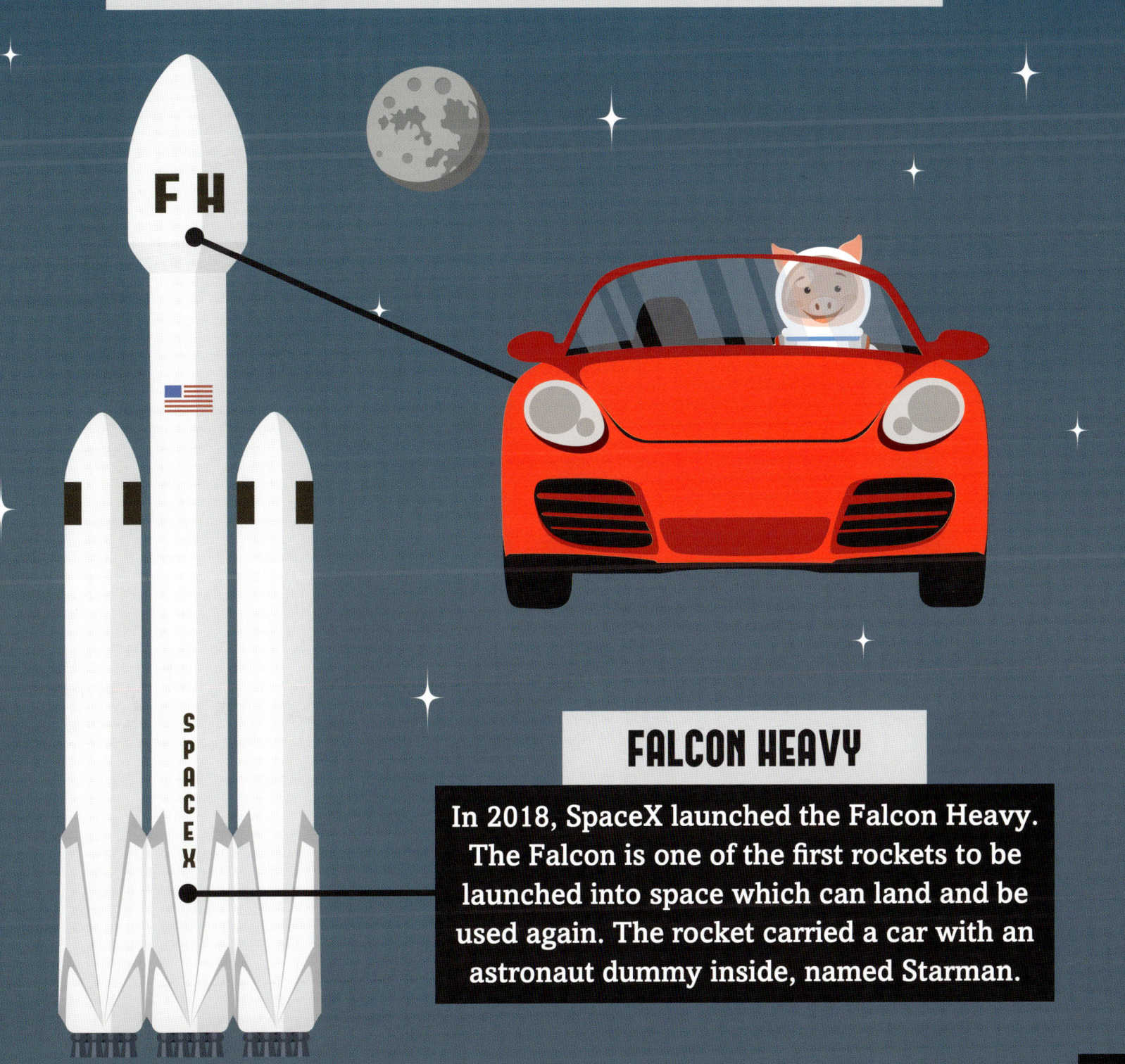

FALCON HEAVY

In 2018, SpaceX launched the Falcon Heavy. The Falcon is one of the first rockets to be launched into space which can land and be used again. The rocket carried a car with an astronaut dummy inside, named Starman.

FLIGHT CHECK

OK, students. Let's test your knowledge about space shuttles and see if you've been paying attention! Get them all right, and you earn your Pink Wings!

Questions

1. What is cargo on a space shuttle called?

2. What is the name of the force that pushes the rocket upwards?

3. What is LEO?

4. At what speed do shuttles land?

5. Who was the first woman to fly in space?

Did you get all the answers right? You did? Well done!

This means you are now an expert astronaut and you have become a member of the world's most elite space force: The Pink Wings!

SPACEWALK!

When in space, sometimes you will need to do repairs or carry out missions. To do this, you will need a special spacesuit to protect you and give you air to breathe...

STEP ONE
Identify Emergency

"SOMEONE BROKE THE SPACE TOILET!"

STEP TWO
Don't Panic

STEP THREE
Attach Rope

GLOSSARY

AIR RESISTANCE — when air resists something moving through it

ASTRONAUTS — people who are trained to fly in a spacecraft

ATMOSPHERE — the mixture of gases that make up the air that surrounds the Earth

ELITE — someone or something that is the best of a group

FORCE — a power or energy

GRAVITY — the force that pulls everything downwards towards the Earth

MANOEUVRE — steer and control a vehicle

INDEX